Reflections on the Political Situation in India

Reflections on the Political Situation in India

With

A Personal Note and Extracts from Indian and English Newspapers etcetra

by

Lajpat Rai

GYAN

Published by

Gyan Publishing House
5, Ansari Road
Daryaganj, New Delhi-110002
Phone: 011-47034999, 9811692060
E-mail: books@gyanbooks.com

Distribution Network
gyanbooks.com
India, USA, Canada, UK, Australia, France

ISBN: 978-81-212-7965-9 (PB)
First Published, 1925

2nd Impression 2023

Printed at: Gyan Press, Delhi.

REFLECTIONS ON THE POLITICAL SITUATION IN INDIA
Author: LAJPAT RAI

Reflections on the Political Situation in India

with

A Personal Note and Extracts from Indian and English Newspapers etcetra

by

Lajpat Rai

PART I.

REFLECTIONS ON THE POLITICAL SITUATION IN INDIA.

DOCTOR SETON WATSON in "What is at stake in the War."

"Our task is nothing less than the regeneration of Europe the vindication of the twin principles of nationality and democracy and the emancipation of subject races from alien Rule."

SIR HENRY CAMPBELL BANNERMAN.

"Good Government can never be a substitute for Self Government."

I.

There are times when silence is as criminal as indiscreet speaking at other times. In my judgement the time has come when the whole truth about the Indian situation should be told to the British public. That is my justification for saying what follows. The personal note appended, will explain the situation perhaps more clearly than general statements. The facts related therein are, in the opinion of many well meaning Britishers and Americans, sufficient to make a man desperate, yet I have never been so, and, God willing do not intend to lose my balance of mind even under more provoking circumstances.

II.

The last ten years have furnished ample evidences of the fact that India, is, as compared with the decade preceding it, seething with discontent, which, not infrequently manifests itself in forms of sedition and violence. That there is unrest, even the British admit. That there is sedition also they do not and can not deny. But they explain away the former and ascribe it to causes other than a general widespread dissatisfaction with British rule. The latter, they maintain, is due to the mischevous propaganda of a few revolutionary malcontents, whose numbers and importance they belittle. But the many repressive and coercive measures, to which they have resorted within the last ten years in order to put down sedition, tell a different tale. The mere existence of statutary provisions for repression and coercion may not mean much, though their enactment in times of admitted unrest, and following the various violent manifestations of sedition, has its own significance. But what is conclusive evidence of the widespread presence of seditionary discontent is the fact that the government should have had to enforce those provisions in many cases. The mere enacting of a Press Act, almost unsurpassed in its comprehensive rigidity and in the summary powers which it gives to the Executive Government, to supress any news paper or publication which the Government may dislike, has not proved effective. The drastic powers given to Government by the legislature have been exercised in hundreds of cases. Hundreds of native newspapers conducted by Hindus, Mohammadans and Sikhs have been summarily dealt with under the Act, resulting in numerous cases, in the discontinuance of the publications concerned and in others, in huge monetary losses to the conductors thereof. Similarly hundreds of other publications have been proscribed and confiscated. Twice within the last eight years the Government was forced to make use of the powers granted to it by a Regulation of the late East India Company to deport Indians of position and education, without trial.* The law of sedition and conspiracy has been changed and altered about half a dozen times within the last eight years with a view to its being made comprehensive, deterrent, and effective. Every time the plea has been, that it was being brought into conformity with English Law on the subject, though it was reluctantly and apologetically admitted that it was also needed to put down sedition that had made its appearance in the country. Even the law as to trials and procedure at trials, has been changed to allow the Government to select its own judges for the trial of political cases, to permit the latter to admit evidence not ordinarily admissible and to deny right of appeal to persons convicted. During the War, of course, even more stringent measures have been taken on the plea that they were necessary for the defence of the realm. Numerous Indians have been interned; numerous arrests have been made. Every letter going to or out of India is opened and numbers of them have been withheld. If a return were called for, showing the number of arrests made for or under suspicion of political crime as well as of the persons and houses and places searched for arms and in connection with political crime, within the last eight years, the figures would make startling disclosures and so also the number of alleged political offender's absconding from justice and the period during which they remained absconding. Violent political

* Since the above was written news have travelled from India that a number of Bengali gentlemen have recently been deported under the same old regulations.

crime made its first appearance in 1908 if we omit the disturbances in the Punjab in 1907. The unrest in the Punjab in 1907 and the disturbances resulting therefrom, were said to be due to agrarian troubles. These agrarian troubles however could be traced to deep rooted economic and political causes. However if we take 1908 as the starting point of violent political crime in India, we might say that in spite of repressive measures and in spite of Lord Morley's Reform Scheme, sedition and political crime in India has not only decreased but has actually increased since then.* It has spread over a large area, has penetrated into the non-educated classes, and has taken bolder and more audacious forms. Violence has been met by violence. Repression, suppression, and consfiscation by secret conspiracy and secret treason. The press has been muzzled; yet secret propaganda goes on. The Criminal intelligence and Criminal Investigation departments have been strengthened and have been abnormally alive and active; private and public espionage is rampant; platform oratary has disappeared; open political propaganda has almost stopped. On the other hand open manifestations of loyalty have increased at least 100 fold perhaps 1000 fold. All this can be put down to the credit of the Government, yet the balance will still be in favour of the seditionists and revolutionists. Lord Hardinge's wise statesmanship has been of the greatest value to the British, but even that has failed to restore peace and establish confidence between the rulers and the ruled. Lord Hardinge's methods have perhaps checked the growth of sedition and its violent manifestations to a certain extent but it can not be

* The Special Commissioners who tried the Lahore Conspiracy Case say in their final judgement. "We know that in 1907 a wave of sedition passed over India, including the Punjab. We know, too, that the wave of sedition has kept ebbing and flowing since then."

said that sedition in India is dead or is dying. At no time within the last seven years has the country been free from sedition. There have been periods of more or less lull but every such interval has been followed by an outbreak of a severer nature than the one preceding it. The war opened with a remarkable and enthusiastic outburst of loyalty. Some people thought at the time that the outburst was neither spontaneous nor genuine but even if it was, no one can deny that it has since cooled down considerably and indications are not wanting that the pendulum is perhaps going the other way. In the war the British had a splendid and God sent opportunity of irrevocably binding India to them and of uprooting sedition, but they have by their policy of mistrust and jingoism, lost it for ever. The policy of trust and goodwill might have killed sedition and created a strong reaction against the revolutionaries and the violent politicals but the policy actually pursued and the cruel and savage sentences given in political cases have reversed the feeling. People are asking "if this is happening during the war, what can we hope for, after the war is over." The war is now more than one year old. Comparing the first six months with the last six months one can judge of the change that has taken place in the feeling both in India and England.* The officials and the loyalists have their own explanations of the conspiracies that have come to light and of the disturbances that have taken place. We shall examine these explanations later on but the facts that (a) that thousands of native Indians have been interned (b) that thousands of arrests have been made in the Punjab, and Bengal, and num-

* We give a few quotations from the Indian Press in the end which should be of interest in connection with this statement, also some extracts from the Morning Post of London, the most influential. Tory paper in the British Empire.

bers in other provinces (c) that Special Tribunals had to be created for the trial of these cases and (d) last but not the least that this time at least units of the army were actually tampered with and had to be executed,* show that (a) unrest in India is not now confined to the intellectuals, (b) that it is not confined to a few (c) that the causes of dissatisfaction are deep seated and fundamental. This is particularly shown by the wholesale loot that went on for a number of days in the South Western districts of the Punjab. . . For a man not biased by pre-disposition or political motives and possessed of a sober temper and a clear mind, the evidence in the conspiracy and dacoity cases tried at Lahore and Multan by the special Tribunals created, under the Defence of India Act by the Executive Government of the Punjab, is full of significance. Standing by themselves perhaps those conspiracies may not be sufficient for a verdict that there is deep seated widespread discontent in the Punjab, but read in the light of past events, of what has been happening in the North West districts of Punjab for the last 10 years, of what happened in 1907, 1910, 1913 and 1914 and comparing all this with the loyalty of the Punjab in the Seventies and eighties, one who knows the province well, cannot but conclude that the Punjab, the recruiting ground of the British Indian army, is seething with discontent.† And what is true of the Punjab, is more or less true of the rest of India. The Punjabees are a virile people, less

---

* 14 have been recently hanged in the Punjab and 4 were hanged at Meerut and 2 at Jhansi.

† The Special Commissioners who tried the Lahore Conspiracy Case, admit that the Conspiracy was "widespread" and that they are not sure if all its ramifications have been discovered but they are satisfied that the bulk of the people are loyal. The Lieutenant Governor says that if not promptly checked "it would have produced in the Province a state of affairs similar to that of Hindustan in the Mutiny of 1857."!!

versed in the art and ways of diplomacy and they can not for long be patient nor can perhaps the Bengalees who are a sentimental people. The causes of discontent, however, that are at the bottom of the political condition of these provinces are more or less of general application. Yet the most important fact in connection with the Government of India is that neither the ruling bureaucracy nor the moderate Indian nationalists admit that discontent is widespread. The extremists among the Anglo Indians and the extremists among the Indians sometimes admit the existence of this widespread discontent but their voices are drowned in the chorus of denials and repudiations made by the authorities, and the moderates among the nationalists. The extremists of the Anglo Indian press want more repression and more brute force in the administration of the country; they deprecate concilation. They have always opposed the extension of representative institutions and the employment of native agency in the higher ranks of officialdom. They are opposed to Council Government and they oppose any further extension of Legislative councils. They do not want any Indians in the higher offices; much less a large number of them. They think that the British forms of justice are unsuited to the country and that the country suffers from over-education. They hold that India was conquered by sword and ought to be held by the sword. In short they are for an absolute, unmitigated despotism. They admit the existence of a widespread discontent, ascribe it to education and lenient administration and want the Government to pursue a policy of repression and extirpation without regard to the principles of law or procedure or the feelings of the people. All talk of leniency and equality is "damned nonsense" in their eyes. Some of them are brutually frank and say that as India belongs to them by virtue of conquest they are entitled to make the most out of it. The rank and file of the official bureaucracy in India think on the same lines, but thé highest among them do not, nor do the Government at home. They would not admit the existence of a widespread and deep seated disaffection in India because that would be a serious reflection on their rule. They do not want the British democracy or the world to know, that their rule in India has been a failure and that the people regard it as tyrranical and oppressive. Thus they belittle these manifestations of sedition, and trace them to the doings and sayings of a set of mischievous revolutionaries, with whom the people at large have no sympathy. They justify their repressive measures directed against the revolutionaries, and they try to conciliate the rest of the country by Homeopathic doses of political concessions, and label them as the "expansion of the liberties of the people of India." The moderates amongst the Indian nationalists admit that the people are discontented but they deny that their discontent is so deep and widespread as to amount to disloyalty. They oppose repressive legislation but when the government confronts them with the details of political crimes and contends that the repressive legislation is directed against the "revolutionaries" only, and as law abiding constitutional reformers it was their duty to help the government in maintaining law and uprooting crime, they are not only silenced but forced to vote with the Government. We thus find a Gokhale supporting a Press Act and a Surrendra Nath Bannerjee voting for a crimes act and other coercive measures. The fact is that inconsistency reigns supreme in all political circles in India and the situation is so perplexing and peculiar that no one can afford to be absolutely frank and speak the whole truth. Consistency in politics, once said Lord Roseberry, could only be maintained by an ass and as the politicians of India (Anglo-Indians and Indians) are not asses, they don't care for consistency. The situation in India is however becoming grave and the fate of both England and India is involved. If England loses India, she loses her rank as a world power but what is even more important is, that she loses the greatest market she has for her goods. On the other hand, Indians are not quite sure that their troubles will end by the severence of their connection with England. The most thoughtful amongst them are inclined to think that perhaps the real troubles will only commence when the British have left India. The British loss of India can be accounted for in two ways; either by another great power taking India or by India becoming independent. So far as the first is concerned a few years before, no Indian entertained the idea of exchanging masters. In his opinion no calamity could be greater and more disastrous than that. The people of India, high and low, loyalists and nationalists were all agreed on that point. But now I am afraid there is no such unanimity even on that question. The Indians travelling abroad have seen American rule in the Phillipines and the Hawaii islands and the French-rule in Indo-China, and through their writings, the Indians at home have also come to know something about the rule of other nations over their possessions and the superiority which in their eyes British rule in this respect possessed as compared with other foreign administrations in the world, has at least dwindled if not disappeared. In some respects the British rule in India is worse than the Russian rule in Turkistan, and much worse than even Czar's in Russia. . . 'On the other point also there is no unanimity. Some of the extremists are inclined to think that no liberty is worth having which is not won by force; that every nation has to pass through a test of blood, before it can establish a free national Government and that a period of anarchy and disorder and bloodshed must precede the establishment of a firm Government of the people for the people, based on law. For them the prospect of years of anarchy, disorder and bloodshed have no terror. There are others, however, who can not look at the thing in that way; they abhor disorder and bloodshed and would rather remain under an alien Government than face anarchy. Then there is the Hindu Mohammadan problem. There are some among the Hindu Nationalists who would prefer a Moslem Government over the British Government but their number is not very large. The bulk of the Hindus would not like Moslem supremacy and *vice versa*. But there are enough indications that the Hindus and Mohammadans are being animated by common patriotism and the feeling is getting stronger and stronger every day that it should not be impossible to evolve a system of national Government which may be acceptable to Hindus and Moslems alike and that in politics, the religious distinctions should be altogether dropped. The feeling however requires time for consolidation and strengthening and this consideration weighs heavily with the Hindu and Mohammadan Nationalists, who though they will love to have India free, do not desire the immediate severence of British connection with India. To this class belongs a large number of thoughtful moderates and in the same category are to be found a good many of thoughtful extremists. In any case it shall not be far from truth to say that their loyalty to England is not actuated by a love of the British Government but by the fears of the immediate future of their country, in case the British have to leave it; yet neither their fears nor their hopes can stop the spread of revolutionary ideas and the expansion and development of the movement for independence. Every death sentence passed by the British Courts of Justice on those who are caught in the revolutionary compaign sends the roots of the movement deeper and deeper and strengthens its foundations.* The sufferings of political convicts and political prisoners are acting as powerful incentives for future action and there seems to be no chance of the movement dying out for want of fresh recruits or for fear. The truth is that all classes of Indians are thoroughly discontented, with the exception of course of those, who are in receipt of large profits by their connection with the British Government. As compared with the total strength of the nation the number of the latter must necessarily be small, and although they exert a certain amount of influence on society and have some following, their influence counts for little so far as the strata of society is concerned from which the revolutionaries get their recruits. A powerful Government with untold resources of wealth and with a large army at its back can always command the allegiance and services of a large number of people who will spy on the movements of their own countrymen and who will hand them over to justice, as soon as they can do so with sure prospects of gain and profit. Once in the hands of the authorities their conviction and punishment follows of course. Every such conviction however adds to the strength of the movement. The convicts become "martyrs" and those who are acquitted begin to actively sympathise with the movement even if they were absolutely indifferent before. Some of them may drift downward and may retire to private life. But there are a good many who become dour and begin to harbour thoughts of revenge. The sufferings and tortures that they have undergone during

* In the Punjab alone within the last eight months from February to September between 50 to 60 youngmen have received death sentences, and a larger number have been transported for life or imprisoned for long periods.

trial wipe out the last traces of loyalty if any, that existed in their thoughts. In any case, their loyalty, disappears for good and they become active and passive opponents of the British rule in India. Thus the number of the enemies of the British ráj in India, is ever on the increase and that of its friends and admirers on the decrease. Those who have once gone through the fire whether convicted or acquitted provide nourishment as well as strength for the growth of the tree which is thus constantly renovated and kept standing. Say what interested politicians (Indians or Anglo Indians) may, there are no signs that the revolutionary movement in India is in any danger of extinction or extirpation or of being appreciably weakened. The reactionaries among the Anglo Indians and British politicians in India as well as in England, whose number is fairly large and who always keep themselves before the public eyes, are the most important allies of the revolutionaries, and so are such moderates and loyalists who speak of the revolutionaries with contempt and ridicule their courage, their patriotism, and their strength. It may require a certain amount of courage to call a man from whom one differs, a coward, but it furnishes a certain incentive to the latter to prove that he is not. The British vilifiers of the Bengalees and their loyalist followers have contributed in no small decree to the evolution of the "Bengalee anarchist." To call a disarmed nation, deprived of all means of offence or defence, a nation of cowards, may be an act of courage and pride on the part of those who indulge in this sort of vilification, but it leaves its sure mark on the souls of the latter and helps materially in the bringing about of gradual transformation which goads them to desperate deeds. Thus every reactionary in Indian politics and every vilifier of the Indian people is a source of indirect strength and inspiration to the revolutionaries and the latter rely upon them for furnishing materials for their propaganda. Under the present state of law, the Indian Press can hardly carry on a campaign of constructive political ideas. They can not even discuss abstract political theories because they may be dangerously suggestive. They can not discuss India's past history because their discussions may be interpreted as veiled sedition. They can not speak of the miseries and troubles of the masses and appeal to them to take steps to have their wrongs righted. No Indian journalist can use the language every day used in Europe and America by Socialists, Republicans, and Democrats against capitalists, bureaucrats, militarists and royalists without running the almost certain risk of being proceeded against under the Press Act. Comments on current topics in the light of past history may bring the writer perilously near the Andammans. The Comrade of Delhi (a mohammadan paper of influence) was proceeded against because it referred to the past history of Egypt—in commenting upon the conduct of Turkey in joining this war. The writer expressed his disapproval of the present action of Turkey but in his discussion referred to certain events that had happened in Egypt in the past. No one could prove that his references were inaccurate or his language incendiary, but the highest British Court, declared that it was sedition to publish such historical truths as might in any way influence the Indians to think disparagingly of the English. Similarly it is out of the question for any Indian in India to try to establish by evidence or argument that the statements made by British historians about the Mutiny of 1857 or about the conduct of the mutineers, are incorrect. Any attempt to defend the rebels or to speak in admiration of their deeds or in extenuation of the charges laid at their door by biased historians may bring the writer within the clutches of the law and afford ground for a sentence of death or transportation for life. While in India, an Indian can hardly carry on any historical research on British administration as it may easily tend to bring the Government into contempt or hatred. Books speaking of British conquest or of British administration in India if published by European or American publishers may be sold in India but their translation into vernacular becomes actionable. A translator of Seeley's expansion of England was once prosecuted for sedition not because the translation was a perversion of the original but because it was likely to create disaffection against the British. A translator of Mr. Bryan's (the American statesman) article on British rule in India was actually convicted of sedition and sentenced to a term of imprisonment. Under these circumstances, it is no wonder that the Indian Press only lives on the mistakes of the English or Anglo-Indian reactionaries—such mistakes as the House of Lords was lately guilty of, in throwing out the Government of India's proposal to grant an Executive Council to the United Provinces. The Indian press was for months excited over the action of the House of Lords in this matter and judging from the amount of space and attention devoted to it, an outsider might have reasonably concluded that the fate of the United Provinces or India, rested on the measure. The measure itself is not of such importance but the Indian politician sees in its rejection, an end of many of his fondly cherished hopes in the direction of a speedy advance in Self Government. If an innocent and harmless measure like that, supported by the Government of India and accepted by the Cabinet could not be carried through, what chance there was, argued the Indian politician, of any measure of real autonomy being conceded to India in the near future. A mistake like that comes very handy to the moderate press, but it is dangerously effective in the hands of the extremists.

It brings fresh recruits to the ranks of the latter; it feeds his movement as fuel feeds fire; it gives him opportunity to ridicule the moderate politics and to pursue his propaganda with renewed force, irresistable logic and fatal success. Thus the movement goes on, finding fresh strength, renewed vitality and driving force day by day. As soon as the courts have disposed of one batch of seditionists, another comes forward and takes up the work of their imprisoned or dead comrades. Outside India, the number of Indians sincerely loyal to the British connection can not exceed, five percent. The Indians outside India belong to all communities, religions and classes and there can be no explanation of their unconcealed disloyalty towards Britain except that British rule in India does not satisfy them and they think that their national backwardness is due to that rule. The contempt with which the other parts of the British Empire and the world outside, treats them, affects them deeply and they begin to feel that life without liberty is not worth living. Indians settled or working in Canada or United States of America are, as a rule, materially much better off outside of India, than they would have been in their own native land. Some of them are owners of landed property. Others have good banking accounts. Every one gets enough to eat and drink and live well and also save some thing for the rainy day. Yet the evidence in the Lahore Conspiracy Case has disclosed how numbers of them left these cheering environments and proceeded to India, practically to give up their lives for the cause of their country's freedom. When put on their trial they made no secret of their mission and openly confessed their love of freedom and have since willingly paid the penalty for that. This is the second case after the Alipore Bomb Case of 1908 in which the accused made no attempt to conceal their hatred for foreign Government and their desire to free their country of it. To a man who had known India of the nineteenth century, this fact is phenómonal. The numerous young men engaged in secret propaganda can not be unaware of the almost hopelessness of immediate results. Their willingness to suffer and to die for the cause of their country, in spite of that knowledge, is symptomatic of the changed attitude of the country and is pregnant with meaning to those who have the intelligence to understand. India has entered on a new phase. Her sons (in thousands and hundreds of thousands) have begun to feel that it is worthwhile to die in the cause of freedom. With 315 millions of their countrymen behind them, they can well afford to die even in millions if thereby they can loosen the bonds of slavery which enchain their country and their countrymen. Large numbers feel that life without liberty is a mere existence but life without honour is even worse. It is a disgrace. Hardly a day passes but when the force of circumstances makes them feel that they are a despised people. Their sense of honor is outraged at every step of their life and they become sullen and discontented. It is extremely painful to see youngmen of great promise, high education, of lofty motives, of noble mien and some of them of the noblest families in the land throwing away their lives, for the merest chance of awakening the country to a sense of shame. It would be a slight to their intelligence to suppose that they entertain any hope of immediate success. Success is not what they aspire after. They die in order to show to their countrymen, the path to liberation. They die because in their judgement there is no other way *now* (under the regime of Press and Seditious Meetings act) to preach patriotism and to exhort people to love their country. Once a country enters that phase, the task of an alien Government becomes impossible. It may linger on for a number of years but its fate is sealed. Oh! how we wish the British Administrators of India would realise that. We are afraid they do not. Else they would not act as they have in the last ten years. What the British statesman ought to realise and once for all is, that it is not in the power of any human agency to set back the hours of the clock and that repression will not succeed where substantial concessions may. The Indian movement has passed that stage when it could be stifled by repression It has entered on a new stage. Once in that stage, no nation can be kept in chains for long. You might exact a heavy toll from people who try to cross the bridge but determined men will cross it, notwithstanding. Nay, they may in the course of the crossing exact a fairly heavy toll of blood from the toll collectors as well. The love of freedom newly awakened in India finds more than ample support from the chronic-poverty from which the Indian masses suffer from day to day. The Britishers' chief boast is the protection they give to the poor against the rich. Yet the increase of crime among the poor due to poverty and ignorance is appalling. The rich often if not always escape punishment because they can buy their freedom but the poor have to suffer and the jails are full of them. The question of the poverty of India and its increase under the British rule has been very ably and exhaustively dealt with by the late Mr. Digby C. I. E. in his book ironically called "Prosperous British India" and by Mr. Dadabhoy Naroji in his book "Un British rule in India." We have no intention of discussing the matter here but we may just note that the British method of estimating the prosperity of the country by trade returns or by the amount of gold imported into the country or by the rise in the price of land is fallacious. The prosperity of a country must be judged by the economic position of the wage earner and judged from that point of view it can be conclusively proved that the wage-earning classes are in effect much poorer today than they were ever before. This is the true explanation of the increase of lawlessness all over the country, particularly in the Punjab. The rise in wages is not always proportionate to the rise in prices and judged by that standard, the wages have actually fallen. In pre-british days the agricultural labour was paid in kind. Now he is paid in cash. This cash does not bring him as much food as he used to get when he was paid in kind. Add to this the change in standards of life and the expenses that have been made necessary by the advent of "civilization." The purchasing power of the Rupee has considerably fallen and that has affected the poor classes most. The fact that the British Government can find recruits for their army on a salary of less than five shillings a week and police conslabulary on a salary of less than four shillings a week shows the economic condition of the masses. Lawlessness in the Punjab is increasing and shall continue to increase as long as the economic position of the masses continues what it is today. The opening of canals and canal colonie have saved the situation only partially. The classes that have mostly benefited from it, are the capitalists or those among the farmers who had some money resources at their back. The peasantry of the North Western Province and of the western and south western districts of the Punjab live in a state of chronic proverty. Their ignorance is colossal. They are unable to defend themselves against the tricks of professional money-lenders. Add to this their religious prejudice against the Hindu. A combination of these three causes (a) abject and grinding poverty (b) iguorance (c) religious fanaticism, explains the outburst of lawlessness in these parts of the Punjab. The outbreak of the war gave only a new point to their ignorance and poverty and they fell upon the unarmed Hindu population (the only people having blood) like wolves. Their readiness to believe that the British rule was over, shows the amount of confidence they repose in the power of the British. They are a virile people physically fit and the prominent among them have arms. Moreover they are in an overhelming majority in those districts. They spare the rich and well to do Mohammadans because the latter have arms and followers. The Hindu trader and money-lender has neither. It is absolute rot to talk of German intrigues or of Turkish influence in connection with these riots and it is equally absurd to say that they were due to the abnormal rise in prices. What happened in the South Western districts on a wholesale scale, in the course of two or three months in the early part of this year, has been taking place in instalments in the North-Western districts for the last ten years.* The Government has so far ignominiously failed to check it. We are disposed to think that the violent crime in the Punjab and in the N. W. Frontier Province will not be checked by the increase of the Police force. The device of imposing temporary punitive police upon an already famishing population is both stupid and cruel. The root causes are political and economic and unless they are removed, the violent crime will not disappear either in the Punjab or from Bengal and will soon make its appearance in other provinces as well. The causes are (a) ignorance (b) poverty (c) want of arms of defence (d) want of training to meet armed and desperate men (e) political despair. These root causes can not be removed except by radical changes in the form, constitution and policy of the Govern-

* The condition of the masses is more or less similar all over the Punjab.

ment. The Hindu leaders of the Punjab are foolish to make it a Hindu-Mohammadan question. The Hindus in the Punjab have been misled throughout by self-seeking leaders. The fact is that they have neither intelligence to probe into the real causes of these troubles nor courage enough to boldly proclaim them. They are working on wrong lines. The Hindu-Sabha in the Punjab professes to be a non-political body, yet it meddles in politics always on the wrong side. As a non-political body it can only foment differences and disunion among the Hindus. It has neither resources nor courage nor even intelligence and wisdom. It is mostly a body of time servers who want to remain in the good books of the Government and to get favours by keeping the Hindus away from politics. The sooner the Hindus realise this, the better for them. Nay the sooner the Government realises this the better for them also perhaps. The revolutionary propaganda in the Punjab owes its virility in part at least to the absence of "legitimate" constitutional political activity in that province. The latter has been made impossible by the repressive and harsh policy of the Punjab Government, who have in this respect been materially helped by the Hindu Sabha and the Muslim League. The political life in the Punjab on Congress lines has been crushed by the oppressive methods of the Punjab Government, the Punjab judiciary, as well as by the denominational jealousies of the province which have been fanned, encouraged and deliberately kept alive and strengthened by Government policy. The sentences passed in political cases and the convictions obtained, in the Punjab, are unique in the history of politcial crime in India.* They have no parallel either in Bengal, or in

* The Bengalee of Calcutta in a most soberly written article commenting on the sentences given in the Lahore Conspiracy Case by the Special Tribunal says that "it would be difficult to find a parrallel to this in our annals of

Bombay or even in Madras or U. P. Yet the Punjab Press* or the Punjab public bodies have not raised even a feeble voice of protest. Persons have been hanged on evidence which would not have been considered sufficient or reliable for conviction anywhere else in India. The last but not the least the Punjab Government have stooped to the most contemptible of Russian methods, in employing *agents provocateurs* for the detection of political crime. Any one who reads the evidence in the Lahore Conspiracy Case can find that out but for facility of reference I take the following from the authorised report of the proceedings of that case. "Liaqat Hussein Khan Deputy Superintendent of Police Amritsar is reported to have said that on February 1915 witness sent for Bela Singh Zaildar of Kohala and told him that he should secure the services of a man who could help them in getting at the returned emigrants and work as a police spy. Bela Singh brought one Kirpal Singh of Barar (informer) and said that the man had spent sometime in the Straits Settlement, knew some of the returned emigrants and would be able to win the confidence of the conspirators through his cousin Balwant Singh, a sowar who was a constant associate of the returned emigrants. Henceforth Kirpal Singh kept witness constantly informed of the doings and movements of the Ghadar party. Witness kept the Deputy Inspector General of Criminal Intelligence Department duly informed of all that............*At witness's suggestion Kirpal Singh had proposed and the conspirators*

---

justice." Similar are the comments of the Amrita Bazar Patrika another leading Calcutta Daily.

* The sentences given in the Lahore Conspiracy Case have proved too much even for the Punjabee Press. The Tribune and the Punjabee have come out with bold protests. The Tribune charactrises them as "shocking" and the comments of the Punjabee are equally outspoken and manly.

agreed to attack the local police station for arms."

The following is the authorised report of the statement of the Police spy Kirpal Singh who had been deputed by Deputy Superintendent Liaqat Hussein Khan............He "made a long statement wherein he explained how he won the confidence of the accused,.........How he entered into their plans and not only took part in their discussion but suggested raids and dacoities in order to get the conspirators together and facilitate their arrest." *

Other witnesses have stated how Kirpal Singh persuaded them to join the conspiracy although they were unwilling to do so or at least reluctant.

If a list of proceedings under the Press Act were called for, it will be found that the Punjab Government's achievements are the greatest, for the simple reason that the Punjab bureaucracy has been the least affected by the changes that India has seen within the last fifty years and the administrative machinery of the Punjab is the most antiquated and reactionary. What the Punjab Goverment has achieved by these methods can better be judged by the abnormal increase in lawlessness, in political crime and in denominational disputes in the Punjab within the last ten years. Lip loyalty and manifestations of loyalty have multiplied, and so also have sedition and discontent. The former has driven the latter underground and made it more dangerous. The Punjab Government has done nothing to uproot the causes. On the other hand they have added to the unrest by enhancement of land tax and, water rate, by their Land Alienation Acts, by their Colonization Acts and

---

*The proceedings of the Special Tribunal were not allowed to be reported in full. The Press was not admitted. A reporter was engaged by the Government who issued a brief statement every day purporting to give the substance of the proceedings. These extracts are from this official report.

Regulations, and by their opposition to the expansion of education.*

It can not be denied that compared with the Government of other provinces, the Punjab administration has been more stupid and reactionary but after all it is only a question of degree. The discontent in India is based on fundamental grounds and unless they are boldly, and in a spirit of true genuine liberal statesmanship handled, there is no chance of India being pacified. The truth is, that India has outgrown the patriarchal form of Government and no policy short of one of complete trust will be of much avail now. The present policy is one of fine and simple despotism, denying the people their fundamental rights. Say what the Governors and others may, the people cannot accept that the policy of the Government is determined for the good of India and that it is in their interests that the present policy should be maintained. The extremists among the Anglo-Indian politicians and the London Times also feel that, and at times make frank admissions which confirm the people in their ideas about their Government. The fact is that India is governed by a handful of white people in the interests of the latter and that this is only possible by denying the people their fundamental rights. The whole

* As an illustration of the statesmanship of the Panjab Govt we give the following extract from a recent speech made by His Honor the Lieutenant Governor. "The comparison has been made between the Revolutionary leaders in the Punjab and the Boer rebels such as De Wet. I have no sympathy with De Wet. He was a rebel and a traitor. One should be just even to a traitor and it should be unjust to place him in the same category as the men whose aims and actions I have described to you. De Wet and his adherents took the field openly as rebels, they carried their lives in their hands and many of them paid the forfeit. Revolution was their end, but wholesale murder, robbery and terrorism were not among their methods nor was the bomb among their weapons."

world is free to keep arms and use arms. Every civilized nation is interested in giving a military training to her boys and citizens and in teaching them the use of arms and other military tactics. Some countries do this by conscription, others do it on a voluntary basis. No Government entitled to be called sane ever thinks of denying arms to such of its people as want to use them for legitimate purposes. The free possession of arms and free training in military tactics for purposes of individual and national defence is the birth right of every son of a mother. Even the Amir of Kabul does not deny that to his people. Nations are vying with each other in their military preparations and in giving military training to their citizens. Even China is thinking of introducing conscription. In Japan military training is compulsory. In some places even the girls learn the use of arms and practise fencing. In the United States as well as in the other states of America the negroes and the American Indians can keep arms and receive military training. But the Indians of India can not keep arms. Every nation is interested in the manufacture of arms and ammunition and in inventing effective methods of dealing with their enemies. Governments give every encouragement to those who invent new arms or improve old ones. All this is denied to the Indians.* Why? because they are a subject people. Their Government can not trust them.

---

* The ludicrous extent to which the prohibition to keep and use arms has been carried will be better illustrated by the following incident reported by the Bengalee of Calcutta.

"A five year old boy of Munshi ganj Road, Kidderpore, had a toy pistol purchased for one anna. On the 8th August last the child was playing with it but could not explode the paper caps. A thirteen years old lad showed him how to do it. The boy was at once arrested by a beat constable and marched off to the Watganj thana with the fire arm. The boy was eventually sent up for trial at Alipur and the Court fined him three rupees."

The strength of the native army in India can not exceed a certain proportion of the British army; they can not handle the artillery; and numerous other restrictions are imposed upon the possession and use of arms by them. Why? Are they not fit to handle arms? Are they not brave? Are they intemperate? No Indian can get a commissioned rank, however high by birth or social position, however fit by education. No Indian can be admitted into a Military College in India or in Great Britain. Why? Are they unfit, or intellectually and physically imbeciles? The truth is that the Government of India not being their *own* Government, they can not be trusted. They can be enrolled as mere soldiers and that only in certain numbers. Beyond that they can not get any military training or military rank. Nor can the civil population be trusted to keep arms much less to manufacture them. Much fuss has been made of the Indians having been allowed to participate in the European War. The Indians have gone mad over the incident as if that was the greatest boon that could be conferred on them. The truth is that the step was actuated by and taken purely in British interests. Without, the Indian contingent, Great Britain could not send a decent expeditionary force to France. The whole of the white army could not be removed from India. In removing large numbers of them, it was necessary to remove proportionately large numbers of the native army also. The British Government is always distrustful of the native army. No amount of false statements and fallacious reasoning can conceal the fact that the British in India can not allow the Indians to manufacture arms or carry arms, cannot give them a military training, can not even keep a large native army (more than double the strength of the permanent British garrison) because, being foreigners they can not trust them. They fear that some day the arms or military training given them, may be used against themselves. Looking at it from their point of view it can not be said that they are not right. But then, why ask the Indians to accept that the Government is national and that they are the equal subjects of the crown; why hide the truth and make false and hypocritical declarations to the contrary? The British know the weakness of their rule in India and in the disarming of the people they see the best gurrantee of the continuance of their rule and power. In the matter of arms, the present situation in India is this. One may steal arms, one may smuggle them; one may illicitly purchase them from those who have the freedom of possessing, for the purpose of commiting crime but one can not have them for defending his life and property, the life and honor of his family (his wife, his mother, his sisters, and his daughters).* It is this which gives awful power to the lawless portions of the society and which explains the losses and hardships of those who have suffered from the depredations of the latter and are suffering from dacoities and robberies and murders in Bengal and Punjab and elsewhere. There are plenty of arms in the country for the criminal but none for the peace loving (who only want them for defensive purposes). All this because the Government of India is a foreign Government who can not trust their subjects and who do not believe in their loyalty. In the light of this fact all talk about the extraordinary outburst of loyalty becomes stale. So long as this state of things

---

* Commenting on the annual report of the issue of licences the Indian press have made similar comments. One of the Punjabee says "while the ruffians bent on crime have been able to secure fire arms by foul means, the law abiding section of the community have for the most part continued helpless owing to the difficulties of obtaining licences for firearms." See also Bengalee of the 6th Oct. 1915.

continues it is useless for the Government to expect that the people can accept it, and treat it, as if it was their own national Government. Never before since the introduction of British rule in India was the sense of helplessness that arises of the consciousness of being a disarmed people, brought home to the people of India so vividly and strongly as during the war. A new fear has dawned on the public mind. "Suppose the British lose, we are lost" says the Indian. The Germans may come or the Russians or even the Amir, we can not even make a show of resistance. All the wisdom and legal arguments of Chandarvarkars or Sinhas will not avail us. A people so helpless and dependent deserve to be despised by the world. The war has made the Indian feel that as a British subject he is really a despicable creature entitled to no consideration at the hands of the other people of the world. Even the negroes (whether in Africa or America) are much better placed than he is. The prayers of Indian C. I. E's and Rai Bahadur's and Khan Bahadur's notwithstanding, the British can not be invincible for ever. The time is to come when their prowess in arms will decay. What will then be the fate of India and Indians. Will they be transferred like sheep? If not actually transferred by agreement, the nation replacing the English in the world power will take possession of India. The very idea is disquieting and crushingly humiliating. But this is not the only circumstance which constantly reminds people that their Government is an alien Government whose interest in them is only secondary.

Let us look at education in India. India has been under British rule now for a century and a half in some parts, for over a century in others and for at least 65 years in the Punjab. Yet the percentage of illiteracy is well nigh 95 percent taking the progress of the whole of India. Greatest ignorance prevails among the peasantry and the military. classes, the two great bulwarks of British rule in India. What has the Government done to educate these classes. Nothing. Some maintain that they have been deliberately kept out of education because once educated they may no longer be such willing tools as they are now.

Agriculture in India as elsewhere is the least paying of industries and it is not at all strange that large numbers of sturdy Punjabees prefer to labour in other countries rather than rot on their farms in the Punjab. In the early years of British rule the educated and the trading classes flourished and became prosperous, but now they are thoroughly discontented. The native traders are no longer happy under British rule (1) because the net work of railways and foreign import and export offices dealing direct with the producer and the consumer have ruined their business (2) because the facilities available to them in the early days of British rule have disappeared (3) because the bureaucracy is always inciting the agricultural and military classes against them and heaping insults on their devoted heads both by word and deed. In almost every province, special legislation has been enacted professedly in the interests of the agricultural classes but really diverted against the Indian trader or money lender. Instead, what has the Government done to open non-agricultural pursuits to them. Nothing. In the whole length and breadth of the country there is not a single Technological Institute. The private or aided Technological Institutes are called by that name only by courtesy. In these days of international trade there is no provision in any of the Indian Universities for the teaching of modern languages. While Germans, Austrians, Italians, Americans and Japanese can learn Hindustanee and English in their own countries in order to further their trade with India, the

Government of India have never given a thought to the necessity of making a provision for the teaching of German, French, Japanese &c. to the Indians and of encouraging Indians to learn these languages. The best part of a boys student life is compulsorily spent in acquiring excellence in the use of the English language. Indians are not supposed to know other languages or to trade with other countries because the English do it for them. It is not the concern of the British to encourage the native to have direct commercial transactions with foreign countries. There is not a single place in India where an Indian student can do real research work in chemistry or other sciences. While the country is full of mines there is no place to learn mining. Hundreds of steamers come and go from Indian ports but there is no place in India where an Indian youth can qualify himself even for merchant marine not to speak of the navy. In the whole of India with its splendid resources there is not a single place where ships can be built. The Indian Government. has never given a thought to these questions because they do not concern them; because they are not interested in the development of the indigenous industries and in raising the status of the people. They have done a lot to encourage the produce of raw materials necessary for their industries or for their food (cotton, wheat oil, seeds etc.) but almost nothing to encourage manufacturing industries. Originally they wanted to preserve the Indian markets for themselves only but their policy of free trade stood in the way and latterly the Germans and now the Japanese are sharing that market with them, but to teach the Indian to manufacture for his own consumption has never entered the thought of those responsible for the administration of India. Perhaps it is not right to say that it never entered their thought. They are too intelligent and shrewd not to know that they had not done their duty to India in these matters but the interest of their own people was paramount and that they could not set a side.

The British Government in India can not go in for universal elementary education as there is a danger of even greater disaffection resulting therefrom; they can not give technical education of a high order as that might interfere with British industries; they can not protect Indian industries for the same reason; they can not provide for real high class commercial education with a teaching of foreign languages and a knowledge of seafaring and navigation as they do not want the Indians to directly engage in oversea trade and contract relations with other nations. They can not protect and subsidise Indian industries as that is opposed to free trade and detrimental to British industries. Yet they want the Indians to believe that the British Government in India is primarily conducted in the interests of India.

The people of India must remain ignorant, illiterate and industrially and commercially dependent because that benefits England and is for the advantage of her people.

But that is not all. The Government of India can not even provide for high class education in sciences, in engineering and in medicine for the simple reason that the higher branches of these professions they want to reserve for their own people. Of late the number of Indians educated and trained in these departments of knowledge in British and other foreign Universities has so increased as to become rather embarrassing to the Government of India. They can not utilise them without reducing the number of Britishers in these services. This they do not desire. The result is that there are numbers of qualified Indians in India with high class British and European qualifications who have to be contented with subordinate positions under Britishers of lesser qualifications, and perhaps at times, of no qualifications. The competitive examinations for higher services are held in England which in itself is a great injustice but this year on account of the war, there being fewer qualified Britishers to compete for these services the Government, has resolved to discontinue some of the examinations, for fear less a larger number of Indians than is desirable, might get into them. Can they still say that the Government of India is as good or perhaps better than a national Government? The truth is that they do not want a larger number of Indians in the higher services because they can not trust them. For the same reason they distrust private educational institutions and insist upon the employment of Britishers as Inspectors of Schools and as professors in the educational service. They will allow a certain number of Indians in the higher offices but that number must not be so large as to make it even remotely possible for them to create trouble for the Government. The same fear underlies the administration of local bodies and the constitution and powers of the councils. It is simply begging the question to argue that Indians are not yet ready or fit for representative Institutions. The real question is the dread of power passing from the Britishers into Indian hands.* It is that dread that is the dominating influence in the policy of the British Government in India. India is a possession and dependency and must be administer-ed in the best interests of the master. Many credulous Indians talk of the liberty loving traditions of the British democracy but they forget that the application of these traditions to India would make such big holes in their safes, purses and incomes that they as men swayed by self-

* Mr. Lowes Dickinson an English Professor who has largely travelled in India has practically admitted the truth of this remark. (P. 23, An Essay on the Civilization of India, China, and Japan, see also P. P. 27 and 28).

interest and love of power and glory, can never think of enforcing these principles in India. The British are good people. In all personal dealings they are honest, frank, and reliable. But when National interests are at stake and the interests of the nation dictate a different line of policy, then, they cannot help following the latter, however, injustice and hardship they may inflict upon others in doing so. The English political moralist and thinker believes and preaches that the State exists for the people; that state and people are really interchangeable words and that the teachings of Trietsche that the state is greater than the people and that the latter exist for the former, is immoral and vicious. In Great Britain and Colonies the British act as they believe but in India they follow the doctrine of the German Professor. The State in India is an authority imposed from without, and is therefore distinct from and independent of the people.* The state in India is the British people and therefore the interests of the latter must override those of the Indian people. Everything in India is judged by that standard. The English may be good, benevolent, just, kind, and fairminded but all these virtues are dominated by the supreme test mentioned above. All the real troubles of India arise from the circumstance. Everything connected with India is looked at from that angle. Unless that angle changes there is no possibility of any such changes taking place in the system and the policy of the Government of India as are likely to satisfy the self-respect of the Indian or to remove the disadvantages from which the country suffers. At the commencement of the war the British politician and publicist talked a great deal of the readjustment of India's relations with England. Even the

* The Pioneer of Allahabad a semi official organ of Anglo-Indians has in a recent issue said that "The safety of the State is and must be of far greater importance than the rights of the individuals."

Tory Press led by the Times made hopeful pronouncements. But the tone has since changed and the intervention of the House of Lords in the matter of the U. P. Executive Council, the decision of the Secretary of State about the Punjab Chief Court, and the constitution of the Coalition Cabinet all point to the conclusion that much can not be built upon the pronouncements made during the early part of the war in the stress of necessity and the exuberance of gratitude for India's "response." * We propose however, to consider briefly the questions that are likely to come up for discussion and decision immediately after the war.

III.

The Indian politicians may roughly be divided into three classes.

(a) The extremists who base their propaganda on fundamental grounds. They do not believe that the British can or will ever grant them freedom of any appreciative kind or any self government worth the name voluntarily. They are therefore opposed to making petitions and sending memorials. Some of them want absolute "Swaraj;" some qualified "Swaraj" on Colonial lines, but every one of them believes that neither is possible except by active revolt or successful passive resistence. They feel that they are not in a position to organise either, for some time to come but that in the meantime it is their duty to do as much as they can, to embarrass the Government by following the tactics of guerilla warfare and by conducting a terrorist campaign. They say they must keep the flag flying no matter how heavy their losses. In their opinion it is the only way to

* What value this response possesses in the eyes of the government classes may be judged from an article of the Morning Post from which we give extracts in the third part of the pamphlet.

carry on their propaganda and make it effective for impressing the country and gaining fresh recruits to their cause. How far they are wise in their plans is another question.

(b) The Moderates of the Indian National Congress who want to conduct their agitation on constitutional lines within the limits of law are not in favour of embarrassing the Government. The men in power in their party can hardly be distinguished from the third party who are loyalists out and out, and are opposed to all agitation leaving every thing to the good sense of the Government. Good many Moderates believe that after the war the Government will make large political concessions and the country will make a material advance on the road to self-government on colonial lines. They have not yet formulated their programme* but the demands that are likely to be made may be classified as below.

(1) Repeal and modification of the Arms Act making it possible, at least for men of education and property, to keep arms without license.

(2) Some provision for the military training of the Indian youths.

(3) Army commissions to Indians.

(4) Improvements in the position and prospects of the Indian soldier.

(5) A change in the constitution of the Imperial Executive Council so as to admit of more than one Indian being appointed to it.

(6) Changes in the legislative Councils.

---

* Since this was written I have seen schemes of Self-Government promulgated by the Congress Committees in the Indian papers. Their burden is autonomy and practical control of Indian affairs by Indians.

(a) Non official, elected majority in the Viceroy's counil.

(b) Direct election.

(c) Removal of restrictions in the choice of candidates.

(d) Freedom of debate.

(e) Freedom from the embargo of the Secretary of State for India, in fiscal legislation.

(7) Similar changes in the Provincial Councils with provincial fiscal autonomy and greater freedom in provincial legislation.

(8) (a) Executive Councils for the provinces that are without them.

(b) A provision that each council should have at least two Indian members.

(c) That the latter should be elected.

(9) Compulsory primary education, with ample provision for Technical, Commercial and Scientific education.

(10) Complete separation of judicial from executive functions with High Courts in place of Chief Courts in the minor provinces also and an extension of jury trials.

(11) Governors in place of Lieut.-Governors and Chief Commissioners in all the provinces.

(12) Exclusive or at least larger employment of Indian agency in the Public Services.

(13) Inaugaration of industries under Government patronage with a protective tariff and ample provision for technical and industrial education in the country.

(14) The holding of simultaneous competitive examinations in India for all branches of the Indian Services for which examinations are held in England.

(15) The repeal of the Indian Press Act and other

coercive and repressive laws put on the statue book within the last 10 years.

(16) Better treatment in the colonies with freedom of travel and emigration or freedom to bar the colonials from holding any positions in India.

(17) Freedom of education.

(18) Local self-government freed of official control from village unions upwards.

Most of these demands will be strongly opposed. Those that touch the fundamental position of the Government as stated before, will be rejected. Minor concessions may be made under heads 3, 4 and 9, and something might be done under 16. These concessions however will not affect the present position, power, and status of the government; nor will they in any way lead to popular control of the Government by the people of India. They will be made in the spirit of kindness and generosity which a master feels towards a servant or slave who has behaved well and served the master with devotion and fidelity. *The fundamental right of the people to manage their own affairs and control their Government will not be accepted or conceded in any way.* How far this will satisfy the people and check the growth of extremism is to be seen. The probabilities are that the situation will become more serious and grave. Even the concessions likely to be granted will according to the practice of the Government of India, take at least ten years to be put into effect and then will commence a fresh struggle on the part of the bureaucracy to make them nugatory and ineffective and to whittle them down to zero point in the actual working of them. Our past experience justifies all these prognostications and we see no reason to assume that the temperament and the nature of the British rulers of India will undergo material and radical changes after the war.

Even now when the war is on and there is acute economic distress in all parts of India and in all ranks of the Indian population below the wealthy, the British services are getting extra war allowances to compensate them for supposed losses caused by refusal of leave etc. and for extra work entailed on account of the war, while nothing substantial has been done for the native subordinate.

Thus the ball goes on and will go on unless something happens which makes the British fear they might lose India altogether. Till then, the Indian patriot may hold his soul in patience and may work for the consolidation of his people. It is an extremly hard struggle in which the Indian patriot is engaged. The odds are all against him. The only thing in his favour is the righteousness of his cause. With patience and sacrifice and the grace of God he may some day succeed though the chances of an early success are few and far between.

(3) The third class consists of those who are out and out loyalists and whom the present arrangement places in a position of advantage. Their number is by no means very large and with the increase of political crime in the country their demands for compensation and rewards for loyalty and services are bound to increase which even a despotic Government will find it impossible to grant. So there is every possibility of large numbers of them throwing in their lot with the others. It may thus be fairly said that in the demand for substantial self-government the country is practically united and any hesitation or refusal to concede is bound to tell very adversely on their loyalty.

So far the English have governed India as if there was no one in the world to contest their right to do as they liked. With the advance of nationalism in India and with the turn the politics have taken in the world at large, the British

Government in India will have to count with numerous disturbing elements. No body can yet forsee the end of the war. Even the best friends of the Allies are not so sure of their eventual victory as they were some months before. In any case the future is gloomy and even the most optimistic can not say that Great Britain will emerge altogether unschathed from the war. Even victory would be awfully costly not only in men and in money but also in prestige and influence. Great Britain won against the Boers but that victory reduced their prestige. The present war is however going to make a still greater change. The Indians can no longer consider the British to be invincible. The Germans have at least shattered that idea and that fact alone is going to affect seriously British rule in India. The Indians who return from the different seats of war will come back with greater faith in their own fighting power, in their strength and in at least their equality with the white. It will be impossible to keep them in inferior positions which they have so far occupied. Last but not the least the Muslim attitude would be entirely different. The talk about ending the war for all times to come is pure and simple non-sense. No one believes it to be possible. In fact there is every possibility of greater complications taking place in European politics as the result of this war. The seeds of future war are being sown and the British will have to be ready for that. A discontented India will be a source of constant danger and weakness and it is for the British statesmanship to decide whether they will like to have a selfgoverning India as a part of the Empire or lose it altogether. That may be taken for certain that the British cannot govern India on the old lines even for the next ten years. No thoughtful Indian at present is anxious or even willing to seek the aid of a foreign Government against the British, but circumstances may change at any moment ending in results disastrous both to England and India. These are matters which we sincerely urge for the consideration of the British statesmen, though we have little hope of their being properly weighed. Jingo Imperialism is a poison which permeats the system, affects the brain, and disables its victims to think soundly. May we hope that the poison has not yet gone deep enough to make recovery impossible. We say so, not in a spirit of insolence but in one of anxious solicitude for our people as well as the Britishers, among whom we count some of our best and dearest friends.

PART II.

PERSONAL NOTE.

The reflections recorded in this leaflet are meant principally for the British public. They are published in this form as in the present state of the Indian Press Law, no Indian publication would publish them and no British publication was likely to do so. The fact that for the last 33 years of my life I have been more or less active in the public life of my country gives me a right to speak out my mind and publish my opinions. In these few paragraphs I desire to relate the sort of life I have been forced to lead since my return from Mandalay, in 1907, where I had been deported without trial in May, the same year. As then predicted by the leading exponent of the Anglo-Indian opinion in India, the Pioneer of Allahabad, in connection with my release, I have been all these years "a marked man." The shadow of the spy and the informer have always been over me, no matter wherever I went. The fear of my arrest, search, and prosecution has always filled the minds of those interested in me because it is well understood that the English in India never admit their mistake and never forgive a man whom they have decided to treat as enemy. Conduct like this would lower their prestige they think. So ever since 1907 I have been treated as a suspect. Every time a political case cropped up I was suspected of complicity and was even more closely watched than before. I never left my house without apprehending that on my return I might find it sorrounded by a Police guard. Immediately on my return from deportation I engaged in famine relief operations which were eminently successful. My appeal for funds was nobly responded to by the country and the Arya Samaj and other public bodies willingly and cheerfully co-operated with me. The operations were, however, greatly hampered by the attitude of the officials and the suspicions under which I laboured. The Government could not openly suppress the movement but their officials did everything possible to discourage it and to stop it. In some districts they even prevented people from accepting relief distributed by my agents. In one place one of my agents was actually arrested; in some others they were threatened by the Collector and District Magisterate; in others again they were persecuted and hampered by the subordinate officials. Yet I managed to give relief in several provinces and the young volunteers working under me did noble work. The work was hardly finished when the head of the Punjab Government and the Higher Officials began to poison the minds of those who worked with me. The latter were advised not to associate with me and so on. The events of 1907 had brought a sad change in the educated Indians of Lahore and elsewhere, and the atmosphere was charged with fear and suspicion. One of the judges of the Chief Court, advised me to resume my work at the bar if I wanted to ward off suspicions which the Government entertained against me. This I was not in a mood to do. So I decided to leave India and went over to England. I was half-minded to leave India for good but I could not stay out for more than six months. (Firstly) because Iwas wanted in India for evidence in the cases I had brought against the Englishman and the Civil and Military Gazette (Secondly) because my father and my family urged me most touchingly to return. So I returned to India in the spring of 1909 and decided to follow the advice given to me by the Chief Court Judge. The same year saw the end of my case against "the Englishman" newspaper which was decided in my favour and I settled down to make money at my profession which was wanted for the education of my son whom I had left in London and also for the prosecution of the other cases against the Civil and Military Gazette of Lahore and the Daily Express of London. I had hardly settled down when the Police one day proclaimed that they had found out highly incriminatory documentary evidence against me in the house search of Bhai Parma Nand. Eventually it was discovered that there was nothing incriminating in these documents and my explanation of certain passages was evidently considered quite satisfactory by all concerned. Still the language of those documents was deemed sufficient to give the authorities an effective handle to create a scare against me. My public activities had already ceased to be of any magnitude but what little was left was threatened by the campaign that was started against me by the officials. The few friends that had stuck to me felt it necessary for their own safety as well as for the safety of their public work and of the institutions in which they were interested to leave me. I was required to retire from all activities connected with the Arya Samaj and irresistable pressure was put on my friend the proprietor of the Punjabee which was considered to be my organ, to transfer the paper only for the price of the press to a syndicate of Hindu Leaders. The step was considered necessary and pressed in the interests of the Hindu Community in general and of the Arya Samaj in particular. The Arya Samaj was then being prosecuted at Patiala and the general belief was that this was being done at the instance of the Punjab Government. Just then I received the news that my son in England had caught consumption and had been transferred to a sanitorium. So once more I left for England and after another stay of six months returned to India with my diseased son. The boy was dying when I was asked to attend the High Court at Calcutta in order to give evidence in my case against the Civil and Military Gazette which had been postponed from time to time sometimes to suit the convenience of the defendant and sometimes my own. It was impossible for me to leave the death bed of my son. So the case was compromised and let drop in default. The boy died and after a few months I again settled down in my profession. At this time I was not engaged in any public activity except some slight work in connection with the education of the depressed classes. The Arya Samaj was closed to me and I myself was refraining from every kind of political work. In this state of things some of my friends suggested that I should enter the Municipal Committee of the city and thus re enter public life. Some titled gentlemen among the Hindus, opposed my candidature and the Punjabee, the paper founded by me, started an active campaign of vilification and opposition. . . As My friends were afraid lest my election may be vetoed by the Punjab government, I wrote a letter to the Deputy Commissioner asking him if the Government was opposed to my election as a Municipal Commissioner as I was not at that time prepared to put myself in conflict with them. In reply, he informed me that the Government was not opposed to my election if the Hindu electors of Lahore thought it best in their interests to return me. This removed the fears of my friends as to the possibility of my election being vetoed but the official opposition to my election was in no way slackened. The Deputy Commissioner of the District did his best to frighten my supporters and, several titled gentlemen and Honorary Magistrates and other officials were kept busy in a campaign against me. The figures at the polls however stunned them and they found to their horror that their machinations had in no way affected my influence with my countrymen. I headed the polls and a record vote was recorded in my favour. So the officials were discomfited and it took them almost two months to make up their minds to make the required announcement in the official Gazette. In the meantime I was favoured with a semi official letter of advice, containing a covert threat, from the commisioner of the division. The letter was written under instructions of the then Lieut-Governor of the Province. I gave a suitable reply. Eventually my election was gazetted and this gave me a fresh start in the public life of the country and although the officials never gave me their confidence and every thing was done to limit my influence in the Municipal Committee, yet within two years from that time I regained my position in the public life of the province and was at the same time doing good business in my profession. In the spring of 1913 I was elected to a seat on the Bar Council of the province by a vote of 28 as gainst 12 but the Chief Court refused to confirm that election. I was informally told that it would be better if I withdrew. No decision was recorded nor any communicated to me in writing. On my enquiring if the attitude of the judges was due to any defect in my professional career or to any suspicion relating to my professional work, I was assured that my professional conduct was considered to be above reproach. Under the circumstances the only possible reason for this action was the fact of my having been deported for political reasons. The news having oozed out, having been published broadcast by my opponents, somewhat affected my practice, as the litigants began to suspect that the judges still disliked me and that their cases, would not be safe in my hands. The bulk of my clients, however stuck to me but the incident disturbed me so much that I made up my mind to retire from the profession. Some private matters however stood in my way. Twice in 1913 I engaged steamer berths for a trip to England but both times had to cancel them. So I postponed my departure to the next summer and continued to work at law. In the meantime I developed my scheme for the elevation and education of the depressed classes and gave away all my professional earnings of the preceding three years to the cause. It was my intention to devote the rest of my life to that cause. The fate however decided otherwise. Just when I was in the midst of a highly successful tour undertaken in the cause of the depressed classes came a bolt from the blue heaven. That was the arrest of a man who had been my personal assistant in that mission for about a year, for complicity in the Lahore Bomb Case (since known as the Delhi Conspiracy Case). The man was not in my service when he was arrested. He had left that service four or five months before, but he was in my service when the bomb was alleged to have been thrown, in May 1913. . . This once more revived suspicion against me and although the police could not find even the smallest bit of evidence against me, yet I was closely watched and every bit of paper connected with the depressed classes movement was searched and looked into. The men who worked under me were harassed and various attempts were made to entangle me. These suspicions etc. affected me very deeply as on account of them I was prevented from helping those whom otherwise I could and would help in their defence. I believed and even now believe that some of the accused originally prosecuted in the Delhi Conspiracy Case, were innocent. I still believe that Balmokand one of the accused since hanged, had nothing to do with the murder with which he was charged. Even the courts, have held that there was no evidence directly connecting him with the incident. He has been convicted and hanged because he was believed to be a member of the society, the members of which committed that deed. Similarly there was no evidence worth the name that Balraj and Hanwant Sahai were ever members of that conspiracy. Both of them have been convicted on mere circumstantial evidence of a very doubtful nature. I very much wanted to defend these people but I could not do so on account of my own position being rather awkward. This made me very miserable. So I waited till the whole evidence of the prosecution was tendered and the preliminary enquiry before the magistrate finished. As soon as this was over I left for England to join the Congress Deputation that had already left. My stay in England and my experiences there made me very pessimistic about the political future of India. I am unable to build largely on the political generosity of the British people. Some how or the other, I can not believe that justice, fairplay, and generosity, play much part in international politics. These latter are in my opinion almost exclusively governed by interest and expediency. I do not believe that England will make any large political concessions to India unless she is sure that the refusal to do so will be more harmful in her interests than their granting of the same. In this respect the ruling democracies are even worse than despotic monarchs. Democracies having party governments have the easiest loopholes to get out of promises and pledges. In politics promises and pledges even, much less vague declarations made in general ambiguous language, do not count for much. Consequently I do not believe that British Government is going to give us our liberties to any appreciable extent after the war, yet I can not bring myself to believe in the sanity of the programme of the Revolutionaries.

Wherever I have been in the United States of America I have tried to remonstrate with them and to show to them the weakness and rather the hopelessness of their methods. Some have refused to listen to me; others have confronted me with the equal hopelessness of the Congress programme and Congress methods and between these I have failed to convince them of the practicability of the latter. The arrest of Bhai Parma Nand in the Lahore Conspiracy Case and the internment of Messrs. Mohammad Ali and Shaukat Ali and the judgement of the Chief Court in the Comrade Case incline me to think that it is impossible for any one at present to do any kind of constructive work in India. I know Bhai Parma Nand as well as any one else does. I know his political views. Knowing these it is impossible for me to believe that he could be party to such an insane conspiracy as the Lahore Conspiracy was; nor there is any evidence to connect him with the latter except the heresay statement of a perjured Police spy. When I left India in April 1914 Parmanand was strongly opposed to all propaganda of violence and said so openly to all those who met him. He distinctly and unambiguously disapproved of the doing of the *Ghadar* party. His History of India gives indications of his being amply conscious of the present incapacity of his countrymen to organise a successful revolt against the British. Under the circumstances it is impossible to believe that he could have joined the impossible conspiracy planned by some of the members of the Ghadar Party. It is possible that some of these people approached him; it is possible that some of them made use of his name but it is impossible to believe that he joined the conspiracy, gave them any direct or indirect help or even authorised them to use his name. He was never so foolish or insane or rash as to be capable of doing that. Yet he has been charged with that and has now been under arrest for the last six months. As I am writing it is not known what orders have been passed in his case but considering the constitution of the commission and the temper and traditions of the Punjab Judiciary it is futile to entertain any hope of his acquitial.* The Punjab Police is almost omnipotent. There are many things done by them which never see the light of the day and can not be proved. Of course the testimony of the victims themselves is of "no value" and independent evidence of torture and other illegal things done by them is never forthcoming. The matter was forcibly brought to the notice of the Parliament in the Gulab Bano Case in which case it was judicially found that the woman was horribly tortured. During the investigation of the Delhi Conspiracy Case some notes appeared in one of the leading papers of Lahore, exposing some of the methods adopted by the Police in the investigation of that case and telling of the pressure that was being exercised to induce people to give evidence. The notes attracted the attention of the Government and instead of instituting enquiries to find out the truth of the statements, the Government lost temper and the District Magistrate sent a ferocious letter to the Editor which stopped all further criticism and exposure of Police methods. I read this letter.

The Police methods and their treatment of the under trial prisoners thus remains a sealed book to the higher authorities but the people know it full well as every thing done by the Police, however secret, leaks out and is circulated from mouth to mouth. Some of these tales are too horrible to be put in words. The methods of torture adopted by them are so ingeniously brutal, and savage as to defy decency itself. The good members of the British

* He has been convicted and sentenced to death !!!

Parliament may cry hoarse and protest as much as they please, the Punjab Police will not give up their methods so long as the officers are recruited from the ranks and so long as the idea prevails that they are not the servants of the public but of the foreign Government and their business is not to protect by the prevention of crime but by obtaining convictions Their prosperity and promotion depends upon the percentage of convictions obtained by them in crimes reported. In political cases the temptations are even greater.

The powers of search vested in them by Law as interpreted by the Punjab Chief Court are unlimited. They can search any one for any suspicion without a warrant or any thing from a Magistrate. But the worst is that their search need not be confined to particular things wanted, nor need they search for specific articles or documents only. They can just search to find anything incriminating and they may remove anything and every thing they like. We have often heard said that an Englishman's house is his castle, but in India no Indian house is safe from the Police and whenever a house is searched by the Police be it for any offence or any suspicion a lot of unnecessary and wanton damage is done to his belongings. The whole house is turned upside down. If the owner has the ill luck of possessing a Library containing books on politics, history etc, he stands the chance of finding most of his valuable books being removed by the Police to enable them to judge at leisure if some of them may not be put in evidence against him at the trial to prove his tendencies or to find out if the books have marginal notes or other marks which may in any way be used for incriminating purposes.* Thus the owner of a library who sometimes

---

* In the search of Principal Hansraj of the D. A. V. College a cart load of his books including University Calendars, Vedas, Upanishdas, and text

lends books to others stands the chance of finding himself in difficulty for marginal notes &c., made by persons other than himself. Great sensation was caused in 1910 upon some letters being found in the possession of Bhai Parma Nand, wherein I had asked him when he was in England to send me some books on Socialism, industrial democracy or dealing with revolutions. I have been fond of books all my life and my collection of books is perhaps one of the two best private collections in the whole Province. I had several thousand volumes in my Library including books on all subjects. When the above mentioned sensation was caused some of my friends became very anxious lest my house be searched and the presence of a good number of books dealing with revolutions and revolutionary propaganda in France, Italy, Russia, England, and Germany, many be used as evidence against me. In their anxiety for my safety and in their zeal for my welfare they removed a large number of good books from my Library, burnt some and concealed others at their discretion thus impoverishing my Library and depriving me of their use and causing me material, mental and moral injury. But this is not all. In India no body's private correspondence is safe as when the Police comes to search they want to read and see everything. Nothing is sacred in the eyes of the Punjab Police; not even your most sacredly private affairs. Having been in public for over 28 years, in 1910, I had several boxes full of private correspondence and other documents preserved for reference including my diaries. My correspondence has been very extensive and comprehensive. All grades of society from the Maharajas down to the Coolies have been in correspondence with me. The highest Government servants among Indians have associated with me. There were docu-

---

books on political economy were removed to the police office. I do not know if they were returned.

ments in my possession which showed the origin, developement and evolution of all the public movements of the province within the last 3 years. Most of them were original documents in the hand writing of the original promoters and founders. All this was extremely valuable material for a history of modern Punjab. During my deportation all these boxes were buried by a friend underground in his own house and handed over to me on my return. I took sometime in sorting them, and kept only such, as were the most valuable for public or historial purposes. In 1910, however, when a search of my house was imminent my friends advised me to remove my papers from my house or to burn them. Not agreeing to the latter course I put them all in one box and gave them over to a friend. A few days after, he very cooly told me that he had burnt the whole lot because he considered that by keeping them he ran even a greater risk than myself. There was nothing in those papers which was incriminating in any way but there was sufficient in them to bring a good many government servants and other loyalists into discredit or disfavour with government for having maintained such intimate relations with me or for having at some stage of their life entertained noble and patriotic ideas. There was again sufficient to ruin the credit or reputation of others. Bhai Parma Nand had when in London, jotted some notes for a future national Government of India on mere slips of paper. These slips of papers were put in and accepted as evidence of his seditious views. Who knew, not even I could remember, how many ideas of that kind or of a similar nature were in my diaries. So my friend argued that it was best in the interest of all concerned to destroy them. I know it as a fact that the correspondence of many a public man in India has met the same fate and numerous documents have been lost for ever which could be of untold value to the future historian of India. It would be thus easily seen that a patriotic Indian can neither keep a good library in his house nor can he trust to the privacy of his apartments for the secrets of his life or those of his friends and associates. On my return from England in 1905 and again on my return from Mandalay in 1907, my countrymen in different parts of the country did me the honour of arranging receptions &c., in my honor and presented me finely worded addresses of welcome or appreciations sometimes in fine caskets. A large number of these addresses were given when I was touring in the country on a mission of famine relief. Instead of carrying them with me from place to place or sending them over to my house I deposited a collection of them with a friend in U.P. For sometime I forgot all about the deposit and when the recollection came to me, and I asked for them I was cooly told that they had been destroyed for fear of being found out in a Police search and being used against him as evidence of association with a "notorious political suspect." From these facts my reader will be able to form some idea of the fear of the police which dominates the minds of educated Indians and the respect which they have for them.

But that is not all. The treatment which an Indian political prisoner receives even when under trial as well as after conviction is too horrible to be called human. It is in some respects worse than what is accorded in Russia. In Russia few political prisoners are kept in solitary cells. In India of late at least almost every political prisoner is kept in a solitary cell from the moment he is arrested up to the time of his release after the expiration of his term. This was not so, a few years before, but the practice is growing now and is the rule, rather the exception. Similarly in Russia as a rule political prisoners are not required to do hard labour. In India the rule is that the hardest possible labour is expected of them. The Russian climate being cold the Russian prisoners do not suffer from that intense pain which is the fate of the Indian prisoner in the summer season in the plains of India when in some places (Lahore is one of them) the temperature ranges between 116 to 122 F. in the shade. Then the food allowed to Indian prisoners in Indian Jails is of the worst possible kind. Outside Jail no Indian even of the poorest class would look at it. The bread contains more than 50 percent of sand or clay. The vegetables are the coarsest possible and cooked most carelessly and revoltingly. Yet driven by hunger the prisoners get accustomed to it and sometimes steal each others food when they find that the quantity given to them is not sufficient to satisfy their need. The clothing is generally full of vermin and bacilli, specially the blankets.* All this is however bearable when compared with the taunts and insults of the warders and jailors and Superintendents. Any one may abuse or insult a political prisoner. The white Superintendent is of course above law and can do any thing. I do not mean to say that as a rule they are bad men. But bad men are as many at least as good men. My own experience was rather unfortunate. In the matter of food and clothing the political prisoners in Russia are sometimes allowed to purchase their own food and clothing. Political prisoners sent to Siberia have much more freedom than is accorded to Indian Political prisoners sent to the Andamans. Yet the British Government, has the reputation of being much more humane and civilised than the Russian Government and the

---

* In this connection I am collecting evidence of those who have personal knowledge of these matters having suffered therefrom and hope to publish the same before very long. I have also been visiting foreign prisons with a view to comparing the conditions therein with conditions in Indian prisons.

British public always talks of Russian methods contemptuously. Russia is charged with barbarism in British circles at home and in Anglo-Saxon circles abroad. An American lady (one of the gentlest and kindest of her sex) who heard some of these things told me that if she were an Indian, she might have done something even worse than throwing bombs &c., and that she wondered at the patience and forbearance of the Indians. My reply was that all this was possible, because of disunion among the Indians and that so long as that existed I saw no good in the throwing of bombs and the killing of English officers here and there and that personally I was opposed to these methods and proceedings. She wondered at my moderation and although she admired me for my humanity, in her heart of hearts she scorned me for imbecility. This personal note should show the British public what a hard lot it is of an Indian who loves his country and wants to serve it. I have written this note in order to give them an idea of the circumstances which produce "Anarchists" and "Bomb throwers." The Indians of all creeds detest taking life even for purposes of food. Yet some of the noblest youngmen of high families are being hanged or transported for throwing or abbeting the throwing of bombs. I do not mean to justify them but I have not the soul to condemn them as ordinary murderers or cut throats. They may be misguided or foolish or insane yet in the eyes of a large number of their countrymen they shall ever live as martyrs for the cause of liberty. May the great God of all, bring about such a change in Indian conditions of life as to stop all this carnage and bloodshed on both sides is the earnest prayer of the writer.

PART III.

(Extracts from the "Bengali" of Calcutta dated September 22nd, 1915.)

THE VICEROY AND THE LAHORE CONSPIRACY CASE.

The judgement has been prounced in the Lahore Conspiracy Case, and we are not guilty of the slightest exaggeration when we say that it has filled the country with a sense of bewilderment. We may be far away from Lahore, but the feeling is universal, and is shared in full measure by the people of Bengal. Of the sixty-one persons, the Commission has sentenced twenty-four to death, twenty-seven to transportation (eleven with a recommendation of mercy), six have been sentenced to various terms of imprisonment, and four have been acquitted. Thus out of a total of sixty-one persons, fifty-one have been sentenced to the highest punishments known to the law. It would be difficult to find a parrallel to this in our annals of Criminal Justice; and the fact has to be borne in mind that the procedure followed was under an extraordinary enactment which dispenses with many of the safeguards of the ordinary Criminal Law.

* * *

The Pioneer in its special pleading for the severity of the Lahore sentences has prefered open revolt to private murder and robbery. It was only the other day that the Allahabad journal pictured state as the most sacred thing on the surface of the earth before whose safety even absolute justice does not count. And today we are told that those who design secret murders ought to be given no quarters while those who lead open rebellion against a State are deserving of mercy.

(From Bengali dated 22nd September, 1915.)

The Anglo-Indian Press appreciates only the negative methods of exorcising anarchism. It is for meeting harshness by harshness and hatred by hatred. The mantra for exorcising an evil spirit is known by the pure in heart alone. The severest possible blow will only scotch and not kill it. It may sound pedantic and impractical, but all the same it is the true antidote to the poison which we are all so anxious to neutralize. The comments of the Anglo-Indian Press on the result of the Lahore Conspiracy Trial are only adding fuel to the fire of popular excitement. It has made the judgement in this particular case the peg on which to hang its wonted denunciation of all classe of public workers in the country. The following paragraphs from a very sensible article in the New India of Madras in which our able contemporary prescribes some positive methods for the cure of the Bomb evil are well worth reproduction. Says New India :—

"The Times of India" in its leader on the conspiracy, makes the sinister statement that it "must influence our form of Government." What does this mean? It looks as though the conspiracy, probably promoted by Germany, which the "Times" admits was frustrated by "the good sense and staunch loyalty of the mass of the people" as well as by "the vigilance of the Police," is to be used as an argument against the Home Rule which India has been asking for thirty years, and is now demanding in no uncertain voice. It is the present form of Government which gives the soil in which conspiracies can be sown. There was much conspiracy in Ireland during the coercion period; it has all vanished with the granting of Home Rule. Anarchical movements can only spread where grevious wrongs exist, and the wise governments suppress them by removing the wrong. It is right for a government to crush a conspiracy, but it is most unwise to use it as a reason for coercing non-conspirators.

(An extract from "Pioneer" of Allahabad an Anglo-Indian paper.)

"The safety of the state is and must be of far greater importance than the rights of the individual."

(An extract from a leading article of the "Times of India" of Bombay an Anglo-Indian paper.)

If this conspiracy had been disclosed in ordinary times, there might have been a tendency to regard the members as representative of a considerable class in India. There is no such danger now. The people of this country have proved their attachment to the Empire by deeds far stronger than any words. The revolutionary party stands out a mere fraction of the population — a dangerous and determined fraction of the population perhaps, yet so small that it cannot command any chance of success whilst the sentiment of the country remains what it has been so splendidly proved to be.

(An extract from "Panjabee" of Lahore dated 22nd September 1915, commenting on the judgement of the Lahore Conspiracy Case. re Bhai Parma Nand. M.A.)

"We have carefully perused the part of the judgement relating to this accused as well as the arguments for and against him during the hearing of the case, and the conclusion to which we have come, and which we think it our duty, with all deference both to the prosecution counsel and the commissioners, to state with the utmost frankness, is that grave as were the charges brought aganist this accused, they were by no means so satisfactorily proved as to make it desirable for the Government to allow the extreme sentence passed on him."

"While the ruffians bent upon crime have been able to secure fire arms by foul means, the law abiding section of the community have for the most part continued helpless owing to the difficulty of obtaining licenses for fire arms."

(Extracts from the speech of the Lieut.-Governor of Punjab delivered on September 25th, 1915 in the Punjab Legislative Council.)

But unfortunately the abnormal conditions caused by the war and high prices, the sudden outburst of lawlessness in South West Punjab last Spring and the Ghadar campaign carried on by certain returned emigrants had let to a great increase of crime in the first half of the present year. Some 800 persons concerned in dacoities had received examplary punishment from the courts, and executive action had been taken by Government against Government officials ailadars, lambardars, and others who had failed in their duty, a strong force of punitive police had been imposed on the localities affected at the cost of those responsible for the disorder...... It is hardly necessary to add that these crimes did, all over the Central Punjab, from November 1914 to July 1915 (and they have not yet ceased) create a state not only of alarm and insecurity but of terror and even panic, and if they had not been promptly checked by the firm hand of authority and the active co-operation of the people would have produced in the Province, as was intended by the conspirators, a state of affairs similar to that of Hindustan in the Munity— paralysis of authority, widespread terrorism and murder not only of the officers of the Government, but of loyal and well disposed subjects.

Leader September 8th 1915.

1914 and 1915.

The not unkindly critics of John Bull have often remarked that he has got a stolid temperament and an unemotional nature. The occasions are few and far between, when he allows himself to be swayed by any strong outburst of passion. One such exception to his general course of conduct was furnished last year at the outbreak of the war...........When Lord Hardinge wired to England the message of India, her ungrudging and whole hearted response to the call of the hour, its announcement in the House of Commons touched the deepest chords in the hearts of Englishmen. For the nonce they let themselves go. There was almost a storm in English emotion. Even the Times thought that it could no longer be in its sulks, it foreshadowed a great change in the relations of India and England. 'Asiaticus' joined the chorus and swelled the paeon of the praise of Indian loyalty. He recanted his creed of former days. He even praised Mr. Tilak. Mr.

Roberts spoke of a change in the angle of vision. Other statesmen and other papers uttered the same language of joy and hope. All this naturally raised hopes in India. Some more imaginative than others, conjured up visions of glory. They imagined they could see the distant gleam of self government. Others again with less imaginative nature thought that if self-government was still a far off adorable dream they might yet see better days. The landing of Indian troops on the European soil was the signal for the outburst of another demonstration of feeling. Their heroic deeds, their unquestioning devotion to duty, formed the theme of sketch writers and leader writers in English press. And yet to any one who had closely followed the course of events during the last six or seven months and studied the writings of the English press and the utterances of notable Englishmen in England and India nothing is more clear than that an ominous reserve has again overtaken the English mind. Mr. Bonar Law talks of a consultation with the colonies, and forgets the very existence of India. Mr. Austen Chamberlain, since the day that he assumed his new office, has put a seal on his lips, and whatever may flow beneath the surface from Downing Street to Delhi or Simla nothing has flown from his lips that can inspire confidence or kindle hope. The House of Lords have already given their reply to a sympathetic Viceroy when in the name of avoiding controversial issues, they shelved the question of Executive Council for these provinces, which is another way of saying that they strangled it. Lord Curzon, Lord MacDonnel and Lord Sydenham are not likely to learn the wisdom which the force of events would teach to more plastic minds. If Indian students in England approach the higher authorities with a prayer that they may be admitted to the Officer's Training Corps, they are told to wait—indefinitely. If Sir

George Scott Robertson, with imprudent enthusiasm, suggests the creation of an Indian guard, he is roundly told that he is impatient 'Asiaticus' has again frankly gone back upon his short lived liberalism, and Sir Valentine Chirol is no better. The House of Lords apparently think that they have done their whole duty to India when they have passed the Government of India Bill and conciliated and respected Indian sentiment when they have apologised somewhat dramatically for retaining the word 'native' instead of Indian in the Act, as if the word Indian instead of the word 'native' would in itself meant a great accession to the political status of the country. Convenience suggests the postponement of discussion on the Indian Budget and the statute allows it. Out here the doctrine of unconditional loyalty is held up to us. We are told that it is a folly, if not a crime, to talk of what may come to Indian when the time for readjustment comes. Meanwhile India speculation, so natural to a nation of speculators, is roaming free. Hopes spring up only to give place to fears.................

There are not wanting men among us also who have only one counsel to give, and that is, wait and see. No doubt the virtues of patience are great, but we think that so far as patience alone is concerned India may easily throw out a challenge to any nation in the world. If India will not help herself she will have little reason to grumble if others will not. Let her distinctly tell England that the time for half measures and gingerly reform has gone and that for bold and courageous steps has come.

Leader September 11th, 1915.

In our article on Sunday on the attitude of British statesmen and publicists towards Indian reform soon after the war broke out and their present attitude of doubtful silence, we said that what India wanted was a position of self-respect in the Empire. We will to-day state at some length the particular reforms that in our judgement needed to be introduced without delay after the conclusion of the war.

The Legislative Councils as they stand at present have to be considerably overhauled. The representation there must not only be larger and wider but more powerful. The shadowy non-official majority of the Legislative Councils must give away to an elective majority resting upon a larger and more direct franchise. The power to control the budgets must be effective and not nominal as at present. The resolutions of the non-official members should be treated as if they were better than mere recommendations which may or may not be accepted by the Government. We have said that the representation should be made wider and larger. This can only be done by organising representative institutions from the bottom. Village Panchayats and DISTRICT COUNCILS MUST BE THE FIRST RUNG of the representative institutions in India. A broader and more active policy in education should replace the present timorous policy. It is all very well for 'responsible' members of the Government to speak of an atmosphere of pure study. Indian opinion, however, maintains that the Indian educational policy is largely controlled by political preconceptions and biases. Indian education must be rescued from its political shackles. Knowledge should be treated as something better than forbidden fruit and not as the source of the evil. Primary education should be made compulsory and free even in a larger measure than Mr. Gokhale urged, for the country has given its verdict unmistakably during the last few years and also realised that the present policy is extremely ineffective. Secondary education should be freed from the restraints which have been multiplying during the last few years. The need for a more liberal policy in higher education must be clearly recognised and the responsibility for it gladly assumed. The closefisted policy which has so far stood in the way of technical and industrial education must be definitely abandoned. In the matter of the public services we do not know what the report of the Public Services Commission has in store for us, but one thing we know clearly and it is this, that if the demand for simultaneous examinations is not conceded and if the lot of the provincial services is not improved, if it is not made easier for Indians to enter the higher imperial services of the country, the Royal Commission must be prepared to face its responsibility for swelling the forces of discontent in the country. The bar sinister which makes it impossible for an Indian, howsoever high and howsoever able, to become the permanent Chief Justice of an Indian High Court should be removed and it should not be considered enough to meet the Indian demand to provide that only one out of the seven members of the Government of India or one out of three or four members of provincial governments shall be Indians. Indian opinion, that is to say, the opinion of that section of the public which can think for itself and which has thought over the Indian problem in all its various aspects, and not the 'opinion of that section which can not think for itself or which is too respectable to express itself in terms of dissent from the official, is quite clear that the steady progress of the country depends upon the Constitution of the Government. The present Constitution has, it is felt, outlived its utility. There is perhaps a time when the concentration of all powers in the hands of a bureaucracy is indispensable for the development and progress of a country. But there are limits to that time......... We ask, is the present constitution of the government where is supreme, one which is suited to the altered conditions of the time, or is it necessary that it should in truth and the permanent official substance, be liberalised by the infusion of a genuine popular element? How this can be best effected is a question on which difference of opinion is permissible. But if we are to follow the course of natural development there would perhaps be not so much difficulty. When Bengal had to be pacified the Government itself fell back upon the precedent of Bombay and Madras and gave it a Governor-in-Council with a Indian Member in it. Why not, therefore, endow other major provinces with Governors, recruited not from the ranks of the sun-dried bureaucracy but from among English statesmen bred up in the free atmosphere of ordered freedom? Why not, again, increase the number of Indians in such Councils? perhaps we shall be told again that efficinency will suffer. But, efficiency is sometimes a commodity which may be purchased too dearly. It may cost at times nothing less than the contentment and satisfaction of an entire people. It will be for English statesmanship to answer these questions just as it is for us to put them.

We have spoken above of the cravings of our soul. They are many and varied, but among them none is stronger or keener than that the nation should be restored to its manhood. The meanest white, even though he be an alien, may bear arms and walk like a proud man on the soil of India. But not so the biggest, the tallest or the highest among us unless he be one whom the Arms Act permits to do so. The self consciousness, the self respect and the dignity which the possession of arms and military training can alone bestow upon a nation, have in all conscience been too long denied to us. Are we to continue to be under a perpetual ban of suspicion and distrust? And are we again to be reminded that we are the equal subjects of King Emperor? Let

British statesmanship ponder over this. What an asset of incalculable value would be the male population of India have been to Empire at this hour of crisis? As it is, the nation can only be a silent spectator of the great drama which is being enacted in so many theatres of the world. If these are some of the changes which India would like to see, no less urgently would she press that her relations with the colonies should be placed on a footing consistent with her position in the Empire. We do not know whether the comradeship in arms of which we hear so much from the Dardanelles or from Flanders would lead to a change in the angle of vision of the colonies. We sincerely trust that it would and that the note which would be struck after the war would be one of harmony and not of discord. But should our hopes be destined to be frustrated then we think the only solution of the difficulty would lie in a system of recipricity which would enable India to deal with them as they would deal with her. For it can not be the perpetual lot of India to supply indentured labour and to put up with inequalities and to suffer indignities. Her position outside must be one, as we have said above, of self-respect.

(An extract from the Bengalee of Calcutta.)

When the war suddenly broke out in Europe there was a great outburst of feeling in India to serve the Empire in any capacity. There was a widespread desire among the more ardent spirits in this country to fight in defense of the Empire and in Bengal, at any rate, there was an eager rush to enlist as volunteers. These youngmen were willing to cast aside their attitude of aloofness from what was primarily England's concern and even of their traditional antipathy against fighting. They set before themselves a new ideal, the ideal of national self-realisation. By their participation in this struggle they felt they would be fighting the battles of their own freedom. They became baptised with a new faith, faith in themselves, faith in the future destiny of their mother country. This spirit of self immolation at the shrine of duty was beyond all praise. It was the highest tribute the Government could expect from the people of this country of their loyalty and devotion to the throne. But the chill air of official scepticism nipped the scheme in the bud. We were told at the time not to embarrass the Government in any way, but we still lived in hopes that some means might be devised which would enable our youngmen to participate in this struggle so that from comradeship in arms there might arise comradeship in life leading to the necessary elevation of our status in the Empire. But a bureaucracy with its instinctive disregard of others' feelings and interests not only threw cold water on its salutary scheme but applied its mind to forging new fetters of repression. Thus the Defence of the Realm Act came to be passed which is far more drastic and stringent than the similar statute in England. Internments have since become the order of the day. The whole thing offers a painful illustration of the psycho logy of the bureaucratic mind in its endavour to breed loyalty and prevent disaffection. For while the spontaneous offer of our people, which was the outcome of a general impulse and of genuine sentiments of loyalty and devotion, has been refused, fresh doses of repression are being applied to the wound thus inflicted on the minds of the people. But the crisis is not yet over, nor has the rising tide of feeling in this country completely subsided. There is a demand for men always for more men, at the front. It seems we cannot have too many men or too much of munitions if we want a crushing victory. All the factories of England—and every available factroy has been utilised for the manufacture of munitions of war—are working at top speed for the production of powder and shells for cannon. As regards men, volunteers are pouring forth from Canada, Australia, New Zealand and the mother country itself, in fact from all parts of the British Empire, except India. Can any one say why this invidious distinction is yet maintained? Why, while gifts of every sort from us are gladly accepted, the most precious gift of all, that of personal service with all the attendant risk that it implies, continues to be so unwelcome? Lord Kitchner is still calling for men. Mr. Bonar Law's recent speech at Shrewsburry indicates that even conscription may have to be resorted to. Why not then accept the offers of our men? The regular troops in the fighting line have earned no end of praise from the highest authorities from the display of their martial qualities. The Abulance Corps shews the latest potentialities in our youngmen that are capable of development under proper guidance and training. We have not slightest doubt that our volunteers would prove themselves equally fit and capable, no matter what the duties they are called upon to discharge. This war is said to be a war of democracy against militarism and autocracy, a holy war of justice and righteouness against the violation of internalional morality and the independence of small nations. Are these asseitions strictly consistent with the refusal of our loyal offer? which also amounts to a denial of equality of status with the rest of the Empire? If, during the heat of the war and in the midst of the crisis, there be yet observed and maintained this patent inequality of treatment and this assertion of racial superiority, how can we expect that they will be altogether forgotten or cast aside after the war when the readjustment comes to be made? Repression we repeat for the hundredth time, is a distintegrating force. It alienates sympathies, destroys union and throws people into hostile camps. Co-operation on the other hand is a healing and cemmenting principle. But without equality of treatment there can not be any co-operation, and without co-operation there can not be any prospect of permanent peace. By accepting our offer the Government may give an earnest of the future reforms and concessions. It will sensibly ease and improve the situation both here and at the front. But bureaucracy has so far failed to realise the situation and avail itself of the opportunity. Let not the words 'too late' be written by the future historian of India of the action of the bureaucracy in this chapter of the history of India.........India wants equality of status with the rest of the Empire and as a means to this end she also wants to fight as volunteers in this war, and if what Burke has said be true of Englishmen, neither the one nor the other of India's claims can be justly denied to her.

(In the course of his article "Sir Ali Imam's speech at the Simla dinner" the Amrita Bazar Patrika in his issue of the 28th September 1915 remarks.)

The prevailing policy of repression, inaugurated by the Government of Lord Minto, is doing unmitigated harm both to the people and the State. It is crushing all manly spirit and creating seething discontent. Every public man who is not in the good graces of the authorities feels that he is not quite safe from the encroachments of the C. I. D. This state of things is as detrimental to the interests of the people as to those of the Government. But, alas, not only has this policy of repression not been supplanted by one of the sympathy and conciliation, but it has been rendered more stringent during these five years............ ..

The Press Act not only sits like a grim spectre on our breasts, but, it reminds the people constantly that the rulers do not trust them, though they have given indisputable proofs of their fervent loyalty to the British Crown again and again, and which have been acknowledged by the responsible rulers, both here and in England, in the warmest terms possible.

(An extract from "India of London.")

In the course of a speech delivered in England Sir Frank Forbes Adam said, "One country alone remained that had not yet obtained self-government—a country that had been called "the brightest gem in the Imperial Crown" and that was India. He had lived many years in India, and during all those years there had been a steady movement towards the day when the inhabitants of India would be able to govern themselves. It might be a long time coming, because there were many peculiarities to be studied, but he had no hesitation in saying that the splendid exhibition of patriotism and loyalty of the princes and peoples of India during the last twelve months made it certain that as soon as the war was over a great effort would be made to advance towards the goal which everyone who loved India had in view."

(Extracts from a speech by Mr. G. S. Arundel.)

THE NEED FOR COMMON SENSE.

If you wish to find out what India stands for at present, go to the utterances of her own statesmen and publicists, and not to the second-hand guesses of foreigners. If you wish to feel the heart of Indian aspiration, read the speeches of Gokhale, of Tilak, of Naoroji, of Ranade, of Ghandi, of

Lajpat Rai, and you will know India better than you could ever know her from the orations of Curzon, or MacDonnell, or Rees, or Hewett. Use your common sense with regard to India, and do not be content to accept at second hand that which you can easily obtain at first hand if only you will take a little trouble..............

THE PARTING OF THE WAYS.

At least be clear on one point. India is determined to have self-government, and whether it is to be self-government within the Empire or outside depends almost entirely upon the wisdom of British statesmen strengthened by British public opinion, and directed by the British sense of justice. Every great Indian, every Indian patriot, is agreed that self-government must come soon. Either Great Britain may give it or India will take it, and those who administer the world are waiting to see if the lesson of the loss of the American colonies has been learned or not. America went because England was selfish and ignorant. Are we at the parting of the ways—shall India follow America, or has Britain grown wiser since 1780?

You will then read what Indian newspapers dare print under the rigour of the Indian Press Act.

(Some extracts from an article from the "Morning Post," London about the loyalty of India and India's claim to representation in the Imperial Conference.)

It will probably be put forward on the ground of being a recognition due to the loyalty that India has displayed and the sacrifices she has undergone in the cause of the Empire. But the loyalty is that of the army—a totally different stratum from the politicians—and the sacrifices are rather hard to discover. Not one penny has been added to the extremely moderate texation of the country since the war began, and a large proportion of the population is unconcious, except through the medium of grotesque rumours, that a state of war exists. The loyalty is in fact of the passive order—with one exception. The Native States which were free agents in the matter, have come forward voluntarily, with scarcely an exception, to the aid of their Sovereign and British Raj through every possible avenue—personal service the offer of their troops, æroplanes, cars, medical assistance, charity—with a zeal that could not be surpassed by any British subject.

(Extracts from an article published in the "New York Times" of October 24, 1915 from an American educationist Mr. A. W. Dulles who has been in India from July 1914 to August 1915.)

Since the outbreak of war in Europe there has been no attempt made to enlist any large number of India's three hundred millions of service. What recruiting there has been has had for its object the keeping of the Indian army up to its normal strength, 150,000, while at the same time England has always kept a large English army in India. The places of the first line troops, which were removed shortly after the war broke out, were immediately taken by territorials who are using India as their training ground and at the same time are kept ready to meet any anti-English movement.

The presence of these Indian troops on the western battle-front of Europe could hardly be considered an expression of the state of Indian opinion even if they went to the war of their own free will. It need hardly be said that they had no choice in the matter. In going they obeyed the order of their English officers, who deal promptly and finally with any suspicion of insubordination on the part of their Indian soldiers; nor was it probably distasteful to them to go, as action is seldom unwelcome to the trained soldier after a long period of inactivity. In action they have shown themselves to be brave and useful soldiers.

Much of the support for the British cause from India has come from the native Princes, the rajahs, who have nominal control over one-third of the territory of India, though only one-sixth of its people and none of the important seaports being comprised in the large territory they govern. At the time of the British conquest of India it was found advisable to keep in power some of the Indian chiefs, who, along with the British, had seized what they could of the disintegrating Mogul Empire. The overwhelming supremacy of the British position left these Princes, whether single or combined, too weak to dream of being successful rivals of the British power.

It will thus be clearly seen that the power of these native Princes depends absolutely upon the good will of the English. Further, the overthrow of that Government in India would shortly be followed by the downfall of the rulers of these native states in the anarchy which would inevitably follow the withdrawal of the English, since the power of these Princes does not come from the support they receive from their subjects.

It does not seem strange that these Indian Princes should vie with each other in their presents to the English Government and should have a vital interest to seeing it bring the war to a successful conclusion. Their loyalty is more often the loyalty of self-interest than that of affection. When we read that Sindhia of Gwalior has given a hundred ambulance cars to the King of England, that the Nizam of Hyderabad has contributed so many lakhs of rupees to the Prince of Wales Fund, you may be sure that these men expect a return on their investment in the form of renewed favors from the English Government and the assurance of its continued supports.

The majority of educated and half-educated Hindus and Mohammedans are not loyal to the British Government.

The loyalty of the lower class of Indian, the laborers, has been alienated to some extent by events which have occurred recently. The Indian workmen in South Africa were so evilly treated by the white element of that country that the condition to which they were reduced became a disgrace to the Empire.